Common Core
Wave

By Carole Marsh
Published by Gallopade International, Inc.
©Carole Marsh/Gallopade
Printed in the U.S.A. (Peachtree City, Georgia)

TABLE OF CONTENTS

G: Includes Graphic Organizer
GO: Graphic Organizer is also available 8½" x 11" online
 download at www.gallopade.com/client/go
(numbers above correspond to the graphic organizer numbers online)

What Are Waves?

Read the text and answer the questions.

A wave is energy that travels from one location to another. All waves come from a source—a force, reaction, vibration, explosion, etc. Waves behave in predictable ways, meaning all waves have similar properties. All waves transfer energy and have wavelength and amplitude. However, there are two different types of waves—mechanical and electromagnetic.

Mechanical waves are waves that travel through a <u>medium</u>. When a wave travels through a medium such as a solid, liquid, or gas, we can see, hear, or feel the wave's movement. For example, imagine a day at the beach. On the ocean's surface, we can see the water swell at the top and sink at the bottom of each wave. When we play music very loudly, we can hear, and sometimes feel, the vibration of the sound waves in the air. And, when a seismic wave travels through the Earth, the ground shifts and we feel the vibrations of an earthquake.

The other type of waves are called <u>electromagnetic waves</u>. They do not need a medium to travel through. That means electromagnetic waves can even travel through space! We cannot see some electromagnetic waves, such as gamma rays, X-rays, or microwaves. However, light, another electromagnetic wave, allows us to see objects and color. Sunlight, firelight, and electric light are all examples of the visible spectrum of electromagnetic waves.

1. Use the text to list three facts about waves.

2. Use the text to give three examples of a <u>medium</u>.

3. A. What is the main idea of this text?
   B. What details from the text support the main idea?

4. According to the text, where do waves come from?

5. How are mechanical waves similar to electromagnetic waves? How are they different?

6. Can sound waves travel through space? Why or why not?

Types of Waves

Use an online resource to research and define mechanical and electromagnetic waves. Complete the Venn diagram by comparing and contrasting the two types of waves.

Electromagnetic Waves

Mechanical Waves

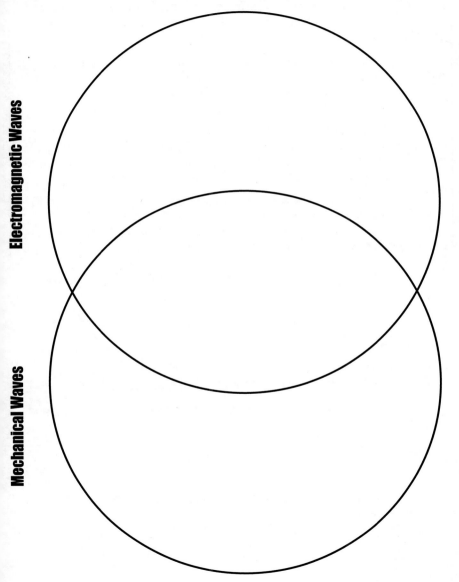

Wavelength

Read the text and answer the questions.

For centuries, scientists observed waves and studied their properties. However, observations can be misleading. If you watch an ocean wave, it looks as though the ocean is moving forward. That is not the case.

When a wave passes through a medium, such as water, it does not move the medium forward. Instead, the wave energy moves the medium up and down. The highest part of a wave is called a <u>crest</u>, while the lowest point of the wave is called a <u>trough</u>.

Scientists who measure waves use the term <u>wavelength</u> to describe the distance between two crests, or two high points, of a wave. Sometimes wavelength is short, and other times the distance between two crests is very far. It all depends on the wave!

In sound waves, short wavelength creates a high note, while a long wavelength creates a low note. In light waves, different wavelengths cause our eyes to see different colors of light. Red has the longest wavelength, and violet has the shortest.

1. According to the text, how does a wave affect the medium it passes through?

2. Use the text to label the <u>crest</u>, <u>trough</u>, and <u>wavelength</u> of this wave.

3. A. How do changes in wavelength affect the light we see?
   B. How do changes in wavelength affect the sound we hear?

4. Use the text and the diagram to draw the wavelengths of red light and violet light.

red
orange
yellow
green
blue
violet

Amplitude

Read the text, look at the graphs of the two sound waves, and answer the questions.

> The measurement of amplitude tells scientists about the *intensity* of a wave. In sound waves and light waves, amplitude is a measurement of loudness and brightness.
>
> When you turn up the volume on your music player, what are you actually doing? Scientifically, you are increasing the amplitude, and the energy, of the sound waves. If you compare sunlight with light from a lamp, sunlight is brighter because its amplitude is higher.
>
> In simple terms, amplitude is the height of a wave. Amplitude is measured from the center of a wave to its highest point (crest) or lowest point (trough).
>
> Generally, when the amplitude of a sound wave increases, its energy, and loudness, increases, too! When light has higher amplitude, the light has more energy, and it is brighter. Often, light with high amplitude can be harmful to people.

A

B

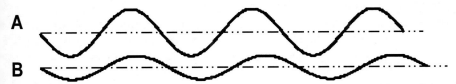

1. What is the relationship between the amplitude of sound waves and loudness?

2. What happens to a light that increases in amplitude?

3. Use the text to draw and label the amplitude of sound waves A and B.

4. Which sound wave is louder—A or B? Cite details from the text and graph to support your answer.

5. If A and B were light waves, which one would be brighter? Explain your answer.

6. Predict what would happen to the loudness of sound wave B if you flattened the amplitude to 0. Explain your conclusion.

Observation at the Beach

Read the text and answer the questions.

My Scientific Observation Journal June 18

Today, I took a trip to the beach. The ocean was calm with small waves continuously rolling on the water. However, near land, the waves grew taller. As the wave moved to the shore, the water rose to a peak and then crashed down.

As I watched the waves, I noticed that ocean waves near land rise, break, and wash up on the shore. I was really curious to figure this out, so I remembered the things I learned about waves in science class:

1. Mechanical waves move energy through a medium.
2. The ocean is a liquid medium.
3. Waves do not move a medium forward, only up and down.

So how could I explain why the waves wash up on the shore? I put two and two together and came up with a hypothesis.

Here is my hypothesis:
As a wave approaches land, the wave becomes squished between land and the water's surface. The wave's energy makes the water rise in a crest. When that wave reaches the shoreline, it no longer has a medium to travel through. The wave energy that usually moves particles up and down has nowhere to go. Therefore, the wave's energy is released as a crash onto the shore.

1. A. What observations does the author make in this journal entry?
   B. What is the author's purpose for listing the things he already knows?

2. What is the scientific purpose in asking questions about observations?

3. What does it mean when the author "put two and two together"?

4. A. Use the text to summarize the author's hypothesis.
   B. Do you agree or disagree with the author's hypothesis? Why or why not?

5. According to the author, what happens to the wave's energy?

Transverse & Longitudinal Waves

Read the text and answer the questions.

All waves move energy from one location to another, but not all waves move in the same way. There are two different types of wave movement through a medium: transverse and longitudinal.

Transverse waves move in a rising and falling motion. As a transverse wave moves through a medium, it moves particles perpendicular to the direction the wave is traveling in an up and down motion.

On the other hand, longitudinal waves move particles in a backward and forward motion, like the coils in a slinky. As a longitudinal wave moves through a medium, it moves particles back and forth in the same direction the wave is travelling. This type of wave squishes particles together and pulls them apart.

Direction of wave travel→

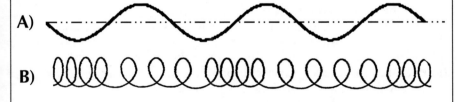

A)

B)

1. Describe the motion of each wave.

2. How are these waves similar? How are they different?

3. Which diagram represents a transverse wave? Which diagram represents a longitudinal wave? Cite evidence from the text to support your answers.

4. A. In small groups, use an online resource to research one example of a transverse wave and one example of a longitudinal wave. Make a list of characteristics of each.
    B. Create a digital presentation including images and text to convey the information. What makes each wave different from the other?
    C. Share your presentation with the class. Then give your classmates an oral quiz on the information you presented. Was your presentation clear and effective? Explain your answer.

Frequency

Read the text and answer the questions.

Frequency is a word scientists use when talking about waves. However, scientists are not the only people who use this word. Your dentist might ask, "How *frequently* do you brush your teeth?" The answer might be twice a day, daily, or even once a week!

Frequency means "how often" something happens. If you mow your lawn once every week, the frequency of mowing your lawn is once per week. If you brush your teeth every morning and night, the frequency is two times per day.

The frequency of a wave is the number of times a crest or trough passes through a given point in a certain time. Waves usually have a frequency measured in hertz (Hz = cycles per second). For example, the crest of a slow-moving wave might pass through a point once per second (1Hz). The crest of a fast-moving wave might pass through a point 30 times per second (30Hz).

One of the main factors affecting frequency is wavelength. The longer the wavelength, the longer it takes for a wave to pass through a point. Radio waves have long wavelength and therefore a low frequency. Conversely, the shorter the wavelength, the less time it takes for a wave to pass through a point. Gamma rays have a short wavelength and therefore a high frequency.

1. A. Give an "everyday" definition of <u>frequency</u>.
   B. Give a scientific definition of frequency as it applies to waves.

2. What is the relationship between wavelength and frequency? Cite evidence from the text to support your conclusion.

3. A. Is the frequency of a wave with a short wavelength usually high or low? Explain.
   B. Is the frequency of a wave with a long wavelength usually high or low? Explain.

4. A. A light flashes 3 times in 1 second. What is the wave's frequency in Hertz?
   B. If a whistle blows every hour, what is the wave's frequency expressed in whistles per day?

CAUSE & EFFECT

Reflection & Refraction

Read the text and answer the questions.

Reflection and refraction are both examples of a wave's change in direction. Reflection is a property you might encounter on a daily basis. When you see your reflection in a mirror, or when you hear your voice echo in an empty hallway—that is wave reflection. How does wave reflection work?

Reflection is the change in direction of a wave, such as light or sound, when it bounces off a barrier. For example, your voice in an empty hall travels through the air. When it meets a wall (solid), it bounces back to you. You hear the reflected sound waves as an echo.

Reflection of light is one of the most important properties on Earth. Reflection of light allows us to see. When a light waves strikes an object it cannot pass through, parts of the light reflect, or bounce off. Our eyes detect this reflection of light and we se the object.

Refraction is the change of direction a wave makes when it enters a new medium. When a wave enters a new medium, it often changes speed, which causes the wave to bend. In short, refraction can be seen as the bending of a wave.

Have you ever looked at a pencil half in water and half out? The pencil appears bent. The light hitting the pencil above the water is traveling at a different speed than the light hitting the pencil in the water. Thus, light refraction causes the pencil to look bent.

1. A. What word from the text best describes <u>reflection</u>?
   B. What word from the text best describes <u>refraction</u>?
   C. Give two examples each of reflection and refraction.

2. A. What causes a wave to reflect?
   B. What effects of reflection can we see?
   C. What effects of reflection can we hear?

3. A. What causes a wave to refract?
   B. In the example of the pencil in water, how is light refracted?
   C. What is the effect of refraction on the pencil?

Sound

Read the text and answer the questions.

Where do sound waves come from?

First, something causes an object to vibrate. When an object vibrates, it transfers energy to the air in the form of sound waves.

When you pluck a guitar string, the string vibrates, releasing sound into the air in the form of sound waves. When you speak, your vocal chords vibrate, releasing energy into the air.

What are the properties of sound waves?

Sound waves have several properties, including wavelength and amplitude. Wavelength controls how high or low a sound is. Some sounds have a high pitch, like the whistle of a bird, and some sounds are very low, like a bass drum.

Sound waves with a short wavelength produce high notes, whereas sound waves with a long wavelength produce low notes. The human voice can create different pitches by changing the wavelength of vibrations in the vocal chords.

Similarly, a sound wave's amplitude controls how loud or soft a sound is. When a sound wave has high amplitude, it produces a very loud sound. In contrast, a sound wave with low amplitude produces a very soft sound.

How do sound waves travel?

Sound waves are mechanical waves, meaning all sound waves must travel through a medium. As sound travels, it spreads out in all directions. Through dry air, sound travels at approximately 340 meters every second—that's 1 mile every 5 seconds!

The further sound travels from the source, the weaker the sound wave gets. In other words, the amplitude decreases as it travels.

How do we hear sound waves?

The human ear is very sensitive. When a sound wave travels into your ear, the wave's energy causes your eardrum to vibrate. You hear the vibrations as sound.

PART A: Use the text to infer whether each statement is **true** or **false**.

_____ A sound wave is a mechanical wave.

_____ When you speak, you are creating vibrations.

_____ To silence a guitar string, you must stop it from vibrating.

_____ The loudness of a sound is determined by its wavelength.

_____ As a sound wave travels, it gets louder and louder.

PART B: Analyze each statement and identify it as either a **cause** or **effect** of sound waves.

_____ Sounds have high and low pitches.

_____ A book falls on the ground.

_____ We can hear music.

_____ Energy from vibrations is transferred through a medium

_____ Your eardrum vibrates.

PART C: Make inferences from the text to answer the questions.

1. Why is it difficult to hear someone who is far away? What information from the text supports your answer?

2. Number the following events in logical order.
   ____ A book falls from your hand.
   ____ You hear a loud noise.
   ____ Your eardrum vibrates.
   ____ Energy travels through the air as a sound wave.
   ____ The book hits the floor, creating vibrations.

PART D: Writing

3. Music is a special form of sound. Your brain hears a series of high and low pitches joined together in a melodic or harmonious way.

   A. In groups, identify at least three different musical instruments and describe the different sounds made by each. Is its pitch high or low?
   B. Use an online resource to write a detailed report on how each instrument creates its unique sound. For example, what causes a trombone to vibrate? How do drums work?
   C. Share your report with the class and discuss. Did certain instruments have common qualities?

Wave Properties

Complete the graphic organizer with the corresponding cause or effect of each prompt.

Cause   Effect

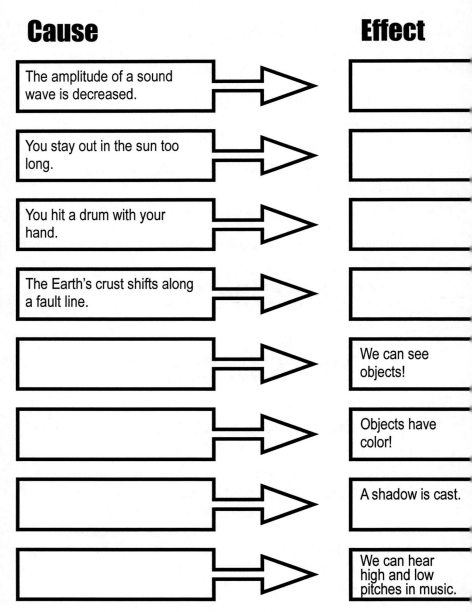

Cause	Effect
The amplitude of a sound wave is decreased.	
You stay out in the sun too long.	
You hit a drum with your hand.	
The Earth's crust shifts along a fault line.	
	We can see objects!
	Objects have color!
	A shadow is cast.
	We can hear high and low pitches in music.

Explain

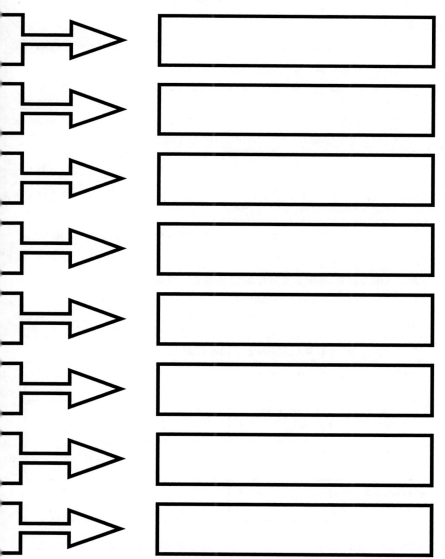

"Ring, Ring! Hello?"

Do the following experiment and answer the questions.

Materials Needed:
• Two paper cups • A roll of string (fishing line or kite string works best) • A sharp pencil • Paper or electronic device to record results • Tape

Procedure:
1. Use the pencil to make a tiny hole in the bottom of each cup.
2. Cut a long piece of string (between 20-50 feet).
3. Thread the string through the hole in each cup, and tie knots on the part of the string inside the cup. Use tape to secure the string.
4. Give a partner one of the cups and keep the other cup. Move far away from each other, until the string is tight between your cups. Make sure the string is not touching other objects.
5. With your partner, one of you speak loudly into your cup while the other holds the other cup to his or her ear. Then switch roles. Record what you observe.

1. First, record the results (your observations) when you listened to your partner speak into the cup.

2. Next, change how the experiment is conducted—see chart of variables—and repeat the experiment. Record your results.

3. Repeat the experiment with a variable of your choice, and record.

	Description	**Results**
Control	As described in the experiment	
Variable 1	Whisper into the cup	
Variable 2	Remove the string	
Variable 3		

4. Use your data to write a short hypothesis about how sound travels.

Words on Sound

Read the texts and answer the questions.

"[Sound] can be both heard and felt. It can even be seen with the mind's eye. It can almost be tasted and smelled. Sound can evoke responses of the five senses. Sound can paint a picture, produce a mood, trigger the senses to remember another time and place... we hear sound with our entire bodies."

—Louis Colaianni

Bang, clang!
Clip and clop,
Sound can be brash,
And begin with a crash!

But pitter, patter,
Whimper and hush,
There's barely a peep,
As sound falls asleep.

Part A: Use the first text to answer the questions.

1. Summarize what the author says about sound.

2. Describe how the author seems to feel about sound.

3. What words would you use to describe the text?

4. How does this text affect your perspective of sound?

5. Identify an example of figurative language used by the author and explain its meaning.

PART B: Use the second text to answer the questions.

6. What words in the text are onomatopoeias (words that sound like the sound they represent)?

7. Cite two examples of personification in the text.

8. Compare and contrast the first stanza with the second stanza.

9. Describe the text's use of rhyme.

10. Identify an example of alliteration used in the text.

PART C: Comparison of sources

11. How are the two texts similar? How are they different?

Wave Vocabulary

Use a dictionary and other resources to complete the graphic organizer for each vocabulary word.

amplitude	mechanical wave	refraction
electromagnetic wave	medium	sound wave
frequency	radio wave	source
light wave	reflection	wavelength

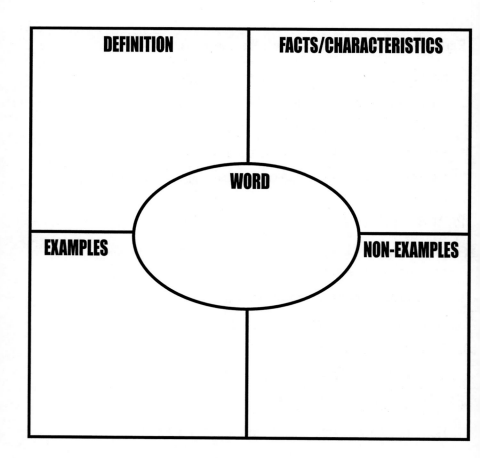

DEFINITION

FACTS/CHARACTERISTICS

WORD

EXAMPLES

NON-EXAMPLES

Light Waves

Read the text and answer the questions.

Light is everywhere we can see. The sun rises and brings daylight. In a dark room, we turn on the light so we can see. Before electricity, people used fire to create light at night. We cannot see light waves, but light waves allow us to see.

What is this thing called light? What is it made of, and what are its properties?

Light is a wave of <u>electromagnetic</u> energy made of tiny particles called photons. These photons are tiny packets of energy that travel together in waves.

Like sound waves, light waves have both wavelength and amplitude. Light waves with different wavelengths appear as different colors. For example, a light wave with a long wavelength appears red, but a light wave with a short wavelength appears violet. Similarly, a light wave with high amplitude is very bright, and a light wave with low amplitude is soft or dull.

Unlike sound waves, light waves travel in a straight line. A single wave of light is called a ray. Because light waves travel in a straight line, an object that blocks light creates a shadow.

Like sound, light can travel through gases, liquids, and some solids. However, light does not need a medium to travel. Light can even travel through space! Light photons are the fastest particles in the universe, traveling at nearly 186,000 miles per second!

1. List at least three key properties of light waves.

2. A. Describe the effect of wavelength on light.
   B. Describe the effect of amplitude on light.

3. What causes shadows? What sentence from the text supports your answer?

4. What can you infer about the word <u>electromagnetic</u> from the two root words "electro" and "magnetic"?

5. Create a Venn diagram to compare and contrast light waves and sound waves.

INTERPRETING VISUAL DATA

Electromagnetic Spectrum

Analyze the chart and answer the questions.

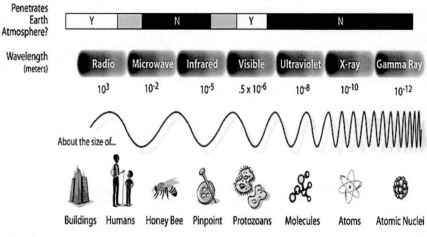

Courtesy of NASA

PART A: Make inferences from the chart to answer the questions.

1. What is the wavelength of ultraviolet light?

2. List two types of electromagnetic waves that penetrate the Earth's atmosphere.

3. Wavelengths are expressed in what unit of measure?

4. What does the honey bee in the chart represent?

5. As the line representing wavelength moves to the right in the chart, are wavelengths getting longer or shorter?

6. Make a guess about the meaning of the gray areas between [Y] and [N].

PART B: Determine whether each statement is **true** or **false**.

7. _____ Radio waves have the longest wavelength.

8. _____ The Earth's atmosphere protects us from all electromagnetic waves.

9. _____ Most electromagnetic waves are visible to humans.

Infrared, Ultraviolet, X-rays & More!

Follow the research and writing prompts.

STEP 1: In small groups, choose one of the following topics for research: radio waves, microwaves, infrared rays, ultraviolet rays, X-rays, or gamma rays.

Use at least two online resources to gather facts about your topic—take notes. Answer all of the following questions plus at least five additional questions of your own.

1) Is it a mechanical wave or an electromagnetic wave?

2) What is the size of its wavelength? Is it visible?

3) Does it penetrate the Earth's atmosphere?

4) What causes this kind of wave?

5) How can we detect this type of wave?

6) A. Does it have any negative effects?
   B. Does it have any positive effects or uses?

Take Notes

STEP 2: Write an informative essay about your topic. Use the notes you took to compose your information into well-organized paragraphs with main ideas and supporting evidence. Proofread and edit your work.

STEP 3: Create an electronic presentation about your topic. Include visuals and be creative.

STEP 4: Give your presentation to your class and discuss. Answer any questions.

Seismic Waves

Read the text and answer the questions.

Seismic waves are waves that travel through the Earth's layers. These "land waves" are mechanical waves, because they travel through a solid medium. Seismic waves are produced by movements in the Earth's crust. When the Earth's crust shifts, breaks, or moves violently, it produces seismic waves that people often feel as earthquakes.

Seismic waves travel outward like ripples on a pond. Some waves, called body waves, travel inside the Earth's rock mantle. Other seismic waves, called surface waves, travel on the Earth's surface. Like all waves, seismic waves have the properties of amplitude and wavelength.

Body waves are the least destructive type of waves in an earthquake. Because body waves move through the inside of the Earth, they often move the Earth in a shaking motion, or feel like a sudden "thud." These waves have lower amplitudes than surface waves and are less powerful. They also have shorter wavelengths than surface waves. They move quickly, and are often felt as the first shakings of an earthquake.

In contrast, surface waves move the Earth's surface up and down like a wave on the ocean, causing most of the destruction that occurs in an earthquake. Surface waves have larger amplitudes than body waves and are more powerful, but they move slowly because they have longer wavelengths. Surface waves cause the earth to roll and even break apart.

1. Why are seismic waves classified as mechanical waves?

2. What causes seismic waves? Where do they occur?

3. Compare and contrast surface waves with body waves.

4. What is the relationship between a seismic wave's amplitude and its power? Cite evidence from the text to support your response.

5. What is the relationship between a seismic wave's wavelength and its speed? Cite evidence from the text to support your response.

Mapping Seismic Activity

Read the text, analyze the map, and answer the questions.

> Scientists called seismologists study seismic waves. They use seismographs that detect the amplitude of seismic waves moving through the Earth. Seismic hazard zones are those areas of the Earth at greatest risk for earthquakes based on the number of times each area has been hit by seismic waves in the past.

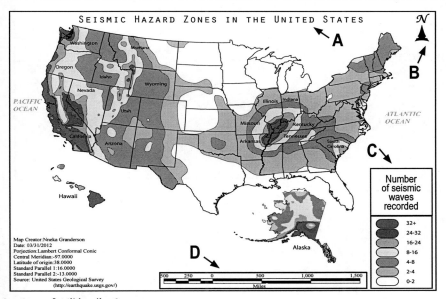

Courtesy of Wikimedia Commons

1. List the name and purpose of each item marked A, B, C, and D.

2. How do scientists detect seismic waves?

3. Identify the regions of the United States that are most likely to experience seismic waves.

4. A.   How many times has where you live been hit by seismic waves in the past?
   B.   How would you rank your risk for future seismic wave activity? Explain.

Parts of a Wave

Use a dictionary or other resources to complete the graphic organizer for each vocabulary word. Then use each word's definition to identify it on the diagram.

Parts of a Wave

amplitude

crest

period

trough

wavelength

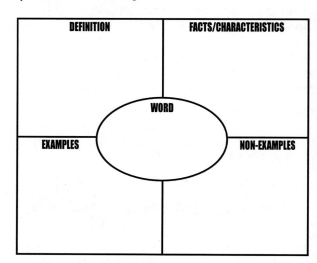

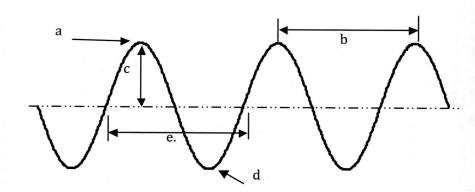

a) _____   d) _____

b) _____   e) _____

c) _____

Waves in Technology

Use your knowledge and an additional resource as needed to complete the graphic organizer with examples of technology that uses waves. For each, list the technology and the type of wave it uses. For example, sonar uses sound waves.

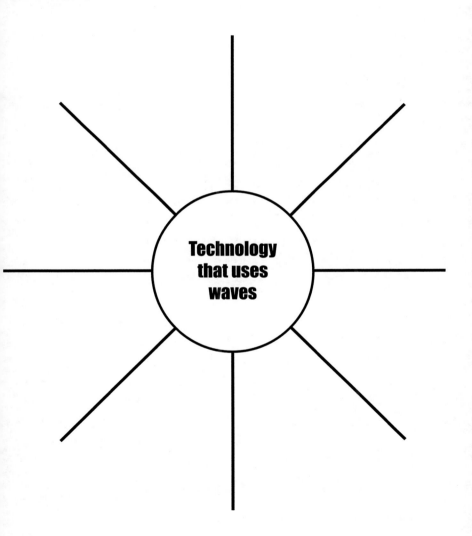

Correlations to Common Core State Standards

For your convenience, correlations are listed page-by-page, and for the entire book!

This book is correlated to the Common Core State Standards for English Language Arts grades 3-8, and to Common Core State Standards for Literacy in History, Science, & Technological Subjects grades 6-8.

Correlations are highlighted in gray.

	READING	WRITING	LANGUAGE	SPEAKING & LISTENING
	Includes: RI: Reading Informational Text RST: Reading Science & Technical Subjects	**Includes:** W: Writing WHST: Writing History/Social Studies, Science, & Technical Subjects	**Includes:** L: Language LF: Language Foundational Skills	**Includes:** SL: Speaking & Listening

PAGE #

PAGE #	RI / RST	W / WHST	L / LF	SL
2	RI · 1 2 3 4 5 6 7 8 9 10 / RST	W · 1 2 3 4 5 6 7 8 9 10 / WHST	L · 1 2 3 4 5 6 / LF	SL · 1 2 3 4 5 6
3	RI · 1 2 3 4 5 6 7 8 9 10 / RST	W · 1 2 3 4 5 6 7 8 9 10 / WHST	L · 1 2 3 4 5 6 / LF	SL · 1 2 3 4 5 6
4	RI · 1 2 3 4 5 6 7 8 9 10 / RST	W · 1 2 3 4 5 6 7 8 9 10 / WHST	L · 1 2 3 4 5 6 / LF	SL · 1 2 3 4 5 6
4	RI · 1 2 3 4 5 6 7 8 9 10 / RST	W · 1 2 3 4 5 6 7 8 9 10 / WHST	L · 1 2 3 4 5 6 / LF	SL · 1 2 3 4 5 6
6	RI · 1 2 3 4 5 6 7 8 9 10 / RST	W · 1 2 3 4 5 6 7 8 9 10 / WHST	L · 1 2 3 4 5 6 / LF	SL · 1 2 3 4 5 6
7	RI · 1 2 3 4 5 6 7 8 9 10 / RST	W · 1 2 3 4 5 6 7 8 9 10 / WHST	L · 1 2 3 4 5 6 / LF	SL · 1 2 3 4 5 6
8	RI · 1 2 3 4 5 6 7 8 9 10 / RST	W · 1 2 3 4 5 6 7 8 9 10 / WHST	L · 1 2 3 4 5 6 / LF	SL · 1 2 3 4 5 6
9	RI · 1 2 3 4 5 6 7 8 9 10 / RST	W · 1 2 3 4 5 6 7 8 9 10 / WHST	L · 1 2 3 4 5 6 / LF	SL · 1 2 3 4 5 6
10-11	RI · 1 2 3 4 5 6 7 8 9 10 / RST	W · 1 2 3 4 5 6 7 8 9 10 / WHST	L · 1 2 3 4 5 6 / LF	SL · 1 2 3 4 5 6
12-13	RI · 1 2 3 4 5 6 7 8 9 10 / RST	W · 1 2 3 4 5 6 7 8 9 10 / WHST	L · 1 2 3 4 5 6 / LF	SL · 1 2 3 4 5 6
14	RI · 1 2 3 4 5 6 7 8 9 10 / RST	W · 1 2 3 4 5 6 7 8 9 10 / WHST	L · 1 2 3 4 5 6 / LF	SL · 1 2 3 4 5 6
15	RI · 1 2 3 4 5 6 7 8 9 10 / RST	W · 1 2 3 4 5 6 7 8 9 10 / WHST	L · 1 2 3 4 5 6 / LF	SL · 1 2 3 4 5 6
16	RI · 1 2 3 4 5 6 7 8 9 10 / RST	W · 1 2 3 4 5 6 7 8 9 10 / WHST	L · 1 2 3 4 5 6 / LF	SL · 1 2 3 4 5 6
17	RI · 1 2 3 4 5 6 7 8 9 10 / RST	W · 1 2 3 4 5 6 7 8 9 10 / WHST	L · 1 2 3 4 5 6 / LF	SL · 1 2 3 4 5 6
18	RI · 1 2 3 4 5 6 7 8 9 10 / RST	W · 1 2 3 4 5 6 7 8 9 10 / WHST	L · 1 2 3 4 5 6 / LF	SL · 1 2 3 4 5 6
19	RI · 1 2 3 4 5 6 7 8 9 10 / RST	W · 1 2 3 4 5 6 7 8 9 10 / WHST	L · 1 2 3 4 5 6 / LF	SL · 1 2 3 4 5 6
20	RI · 1 2 3 4 5 6 7 8 9 10 / RST	W · 1 2 3 4 5 6 7 8 9 10 / WHST	L · 1 2 3 4 5 6 / LF	SL · 1 2 3 4 5 6
21	RI · 1 2 3 4 5 6 7 8 9 10 / RST	W · 1 2 3 4 5 6 7 8 9 10 / WHST	L · 1 2 3 4 5 6 / LF	SL · 1 2 3 4 5 6
22	RI · 1 2 3 4 5 6 7 8 9 10 / RST	W · 1 2 3 4 5 6 7 8 9 10 / WHST	L · 1 2 3 4 5 6 / LF	SL · 1 2 3 4 5 6
23	RI · 1 2 3 4 5 6 7 8 9 10 / RST	W · 1 2 3 4 5 6 7 8 9 10 / WHST	L · 1 2 3 4 5 6 / LF	SL · 1 2 3 4 5 6
COMPLETE BOOK	RI · 1 2 3 4 5 6 7 8 9 10 / RST	W · 1 2 3 4 5 6 7 8 9 10 / WHST	L · 1 2 3 4 5 6 / LF	SL · 1 2 3 4 5 6

For the complete Common Core standard identifier, combine your grade + "." + letter code above + "." + number code above.

In addition to the correlations indicated here, the activities may be adapted or expanded to align to additional standards and to meet the diverse needs of your unique students!